First World War
and Army of Occupation
War Diary
France, Belgium and Germany

1 DIVISION
2 Infantry Brigade
Royal Sussex Regiment
1/5 Battalion
16 February 1915 - 29 August 1915

WO95/1269/2

The Naval & Military Press Ltd
www.nmarchive.com
Published in association with The National Archives

Published by

The Naval & Military Press Ltd

Unit 10 Ridgewood Industrial Park,

Uckfield, East Sussex,

TN22 5QE England

Tel: +44 (0) 1825 749494

www.naval-military-press.com

www.nmarchive.com

This diary has been reprinted in facsimile from the original. Any imperfections are inevitably reproduced and the quality may fall short of modern type and cartographic standards.

© **Crown Copyright**
Images reproduced by permission of The National Archives, London, England, 2015.

Contents

Document type	Place/Title	Date From	Date To
Heading	WO95/1269/2		
Heading	2nd Brigade 1st Division France 1/5th Battalion Royal Sussex Regt. 16 Feb-19 Aug 1915		
Heading	1st Div. 2nd Brigade. 5th Battn, The Royal Sussex Regt., Feb 16th-July 31st, 1915		
Heading	2nd Brigade 1/5th Royal Sussex Vol I 16.2-31.3.15		
War Diary	Emret of London	16/02/1915	18/02/1915
War Diary	Southampton Le Havre	19/02/1915	20/02/1915
War Diary	Allouagne	21/02/1915	26/02/1915
War Diary	Hingette	27/02/1915	02/03/1915
War Diary	Ecornet Mald	10/03/1915	10/03/1915
War Diary	Les Facons	12/03/1915	12/03/1915
War Diary	Hingette	13/03/1915	13/03/1915
War Diary	Gorre	14/03/1915	17/03/1915
War Diary	Festubert	18/03/1915	22/03/1915
War Diary	Le Touret	23/03/1915	26/03/1915
War Diary	Richebourg L'Avoue	27/03/1915	30/03/1915
War Diary	Hingette	31/03/1915	31/03/1915
Heading	1st Division 2nd Brigade 5th Royal Sussex Vol II 1-30th April		
War Diary	Hingette	01/04/1915	01/04/1915
War Diary	Neuve Chapelle	07/04/1915	11/04/1915
War Diary	Richebourg St Vaast	12/04/1915	12/04/1915
War Diary	Gonnehem	13/04/1915	13/04/1915
War Diary	Long Cornet	24/04/1915	26/04/1915
War Diary	Richebourg St Vaast	27/04/1915	27/04/1915
War Diary	Richebourg L'Avoue	28/04/1915	30/04/1915
Heading	2nd Brigade. 5th Royal Sussex Vol III 1-31.5.15		
War Diary	Richebourg L'Avoue	01/05/1915	02/05/1915
War Diary	Gonnehem	03/05/1915	03/05/1915
War Diary	Mesplaux	06/05/1915	07/05/1915
War Diary	Richebourg L'Avoue	08/05/1915	09/05/1915
War Diary	Avelette	10/05/1915	10/05/1915
War Diary	Gonnehem	11/05/1915	11/05/1915
War Diary	Bethune	12/05/1915	12/05/1915
War Diary	Cambrin	20/05/1915	31/05/1915
Diagram etc	Attack Plan 5th R Sussex Reg.		
Heading	2nd Division 1/5th Sussex Vol IV 1-27.6.15		
War Diary	Cuinchy	01/06/1915	01/06/1915
War Diary	La Beuvriere	04/06/1915	08/06/1915
War Diary	Quesnoy	16/06/1915	16/06/1915
War Diary	Verquin	19/06/1915	19/06/1915
War Diary	Allouagne	24/06/1915	26/06/1915
War Diary	Verquignieul	27/06/1915	27/06/1915
Heading	1st Division 1/5th R. Sussex Vol V 1-31.7.15		
War Diary	Verquingneul	01/07/1915	01/07/1915
War Diary	Cambrin	07/07/1915	07/07/1915
War Diary	Verquin	13/07/1915	13/07/1915
War Diary	Vermelles	19/07/1915	22/07/1915
War Diary	La Bourse	25/07/1915	27/07/1915

War Diary	Garden City	31/07/1915	01/08/1915
War Diary	Sailly La Bourse	06/08/1915	06/08/1915
War Diary	Cambrin	08/08/1915	08/08/1915
War Diary	Aknequin	12/08/1915	17/08/1915
War Diary	Fouqverevil	18/08/1915	19/09/1915
War Diary	Doullens	20/09/1915	20/09/1915
War Diary	Sarton	21/08/1915	21/08/1915
War Diary	Louvencourt	21/08/1915	25/08/1915
War Diary	Sailly-Au-Bois	29/08/1915	29/08/1915
Heading	5/Royal Sussex August 1915		
Heading	France 5 Bn 2 Battn 1st Div 16 Feb 19 Aug 1915		

WO 95/12692

WO 95/12692

2ND BRIGADE
1ST DIVISION

FRANCE
1/5TH BATTALION
ROYAL SUSSEX REGT.
16 FEB – 19 AUG 1915

To 48 DIVISION (PIONEERS)

Index

SUBJECT.

1ST DIV

No.	Contents.	Date.

2ND BRIGADE,

5TH BATT'N,

The ROYAL SUSSEX REG'T,

FEB 16TH – JULY 31ST, 1915

121/48/4

C.1

2nd Brigade
―
1/5th Royal Sussex
―――
Vol I 16.2. — 31.3.15

WAR DIARY
INTELLIGENCE SUMMARY
(Erase heading not required.)

Army Form C. 2118.

Instructions regarding War Diaries and Intelligence Summaries are contained in F.S. Regs., Part II. and the Staff Manual respectively. Title pages will be prepared in manuscript.

Place	Date	Hour	Summary of Events and Information	Remarks and references to Appendices
Eastern Flanders	16.2.15	10.30 am	The Battalion was inspected by General Hornsk preparatory to receiving orders for its further Preparatory Training. Orders received 5 p.m. ready to entrain on 18th inst. at time to be notified later.	
	—	2.15 p.m		
	18.2.15	8.20 pm	The Battalion commenced entrainment at Nebuto for Southampton.	
		6 p.m	Entrained in S.S. "Pancras" — sailed.	
Southampton Le Havre	19.2.15	4 a.m	Arrived off Le Havre — stood to till about mid-day. — Disembarkation was completed by about 3 p.m. The Battalion marched to No 1 Rest Camp on hills above St Adresse.	
	20.2.15	7 p.m	Entrained.	
Morogues	21.2.15	9 p.m	Arrived here after de-training at Chocques & marched into Billets — Major Hobbs sent to Sheffield & Lillers. Battalion & 2nd Ingsns — 11th Brigade with 2/Hampton, 2/K.R.R., & 1/2 N. Lancs under first Reinforcements.	
	27.2.15		Orders received from Hinges on 25th inst.	
	27.2.15	11.30 am	Inspection of the Battalion by G.O.C. 1st Army Corps. Orders received to move to Hinges's tomorrow.	
Hingette	28.2.15	2.45 pm	Marched here, via Chocques, Vendin-Lez-Bethune, to Hinges — thence about 2 miles — Took over billets on left side of Canal.	
	2.3.15		Moved out of billets east side of Canal to attack our men some at Avelette.	
E Cornet Malo	10.3.15	7.15 am	Marched to Le Carret Malo — stood by all day. The Brigade in Army Reserve during attack on Neuve Chapelle — Took up billets for the night.	
Les Facons	12.3.15	7.30 pm	Marched here & took up front billets — my show —	
Hingette	13.3.15		Moved back here by marching behind the Gents's trenches — Battalion with transport complete moved off in 11 minutes after receipt of order to move.	
Gorre	14.3.15		Watched wire & took up billets in support in supt shelter. L.K. trenches in front of Festubert.	
	15.3.15		Working parties sent up after dark — [Self & 2 company] officers into 2nd A's to learn about it.	
	17.3.15		Three men of transport hit by 17 Queens when inserving 5 Forster. Show several wounded in shelter — Battalion is next whilst supplying working party is Kennedy. Pte Mushett 1730 wounded in armpit.	

Bishop slightly [illegible]

Army Form C. 2118.

WAR DIARY
or
INTELLIGENCE SUMMARY.
(Erase heading not required.)

Instructions regarding War Diaries and Intelligence Summaries are contained in F.S. Regs., Part II. and the Staff Manual respectively. Title pages will be prepared in manuscript.

Place	Date	Hour	Summary of Events and Information	Remarks and references to Appendices
FESTUBERT	18/3/15	7 p.m.	Took over Hd 22 & trenches from 2nd Batt; C & D Companies in trenches - one platoon of A Co in note "F" - remainder in second series. Hd Co in 1st Reserve in FESTUBERT village.	
"	19.3.15		Pte P.M.J. Vinac - 2375 "C" Coy killed - not though hue.	
"	20.3.15		Trench Companies relieved - Last platoon of A platoon of 9 in - 2644 Pte Catt B. killed. Ptes Adams, Browne, Almeter wounded - the Latter severely	
"	22.3.15		Handed over trenches to 1/WORCESTER Regt. [Lce Cpl Casers wounded] marched to BILLETS at PONT TOURNANT near LOCON.	
LE TOURET	23.3.15		Marched back & took up billets in support of 2nd Division in trenches near RUE DU BOIS - South of RICHEBOURG St.	
"	24.3.15		"C" "D" Companies sent on a detachment under Major Langham & VAAST, in vicinity in support of trenches.	
"	26.3.15	11.30 a.m	Orders received to take hour of duty in trenches tomorrow.	
RICHEBOURG L'AVOUÉ	27.3.15	7 p.m.	Relieved 2/Sussex in trenches - A. B. C. Companies in trenches. D Coy in support. Whilst relief in prog. "A" Coy being wiped & often down.	5/25
"	28.3.15		[Casualties - Pte J. Wair & Garner ("A" Company) killed by shell bursting in their mat. Pte Taylor & Hayward killed by rifle fire in advanced trench - 2 men wounded] Johnson trustrant completed by 3.0 pm. also rifle pits & 5'x 2' trench.	
"	29.3.15		Advanced trenches completed - loophules in left of our left section in order - To keep line there pantre looking after his two heated - "B" Company severely attack twenty minutes later of lights. Communication trench into centre section commenced at 10 p.m. 2 Platoons of "B" Co in centre trench.	
"	30.3.15		[Cpl. Garnaghan & Pte Tester "B" Coy Killed by rifle fire in] Retirement trench which is now my line about two squadrons of dragoons - Relieved at 10 p.m. by 1st Gloucestershire Regts, marched to Companies at HINGETTE.	

Army Form C. 2118.

WAR DIARY
or
INTELLIGENCE SUMMARY.

(Erase heading not required.)

Instructions regarding War Diaries and Intelligence Summaries are contained in F. S. Regs., Part II. and the Staff Manual respectively. Title pages will be prepared in manuscript.

Place	Date	Hour	Summary of Events and Information	Remarks and references to Appendices
ANGETTE	31.3.15	4.30 am	Move completed. No casualties during relief. At rest during day.	

F.W.S. Vaughan Lt Col.
S.R. Sussex Regt.

C.2

12/5/16

1st Division.
2 Brigade.

5th Royal Sussex.

Vol II — 30th April.

Army Form C. 2118.

WAR DIARY
or
INTELLIGENCE SUMMARY.
(Erase heading not required.)

Instructions regarding War Diaries and Intelligence Summaries are contained in F.S. Regs., Part II. and the Staff Manual respectively. Title pages will be prepared in manuscript.

Place	Date	Hour	Summary of Events and Information	Remarks and references to Appendices
ABOUT HINGETTE	3.4.15		In rest billets — until	
NEUVE CHAPELLE	3.4.15		Orders known up to trenches have this evening — "A" Company in Brigade Reserve at PRIMEUSQUE St VAAST; "B" & "D" C in D'AYS in trenches from right half from road K730 15 to A162 North of PORT ARTHUR to the Brewery — trenches there are 8-500 yards apart and not on left "C" Company, whose trenches about 250 yards	3/35
	2.4.15		Capt. T.B. Hawthorn wounded whilst inspecting early morning wire inspection.	
	11.4.15		"D" Comp. relieved by 4th Suffolks; 16th Welch in PICANTLOYPE St VAAST. Proceeded during [last 3 days] in ambulances during trip's trip for shelling; no casualties about 30 officers.	
RICHEBOURG St VAAST	12.4.15		"B" & "C" Comps. relieved by 2/ 2nd Gurkhas — Rltd at Rue D'OUVERT — "A" & "D" Coys. to GONNEHEM.	
GONNEHEM	13.4.15		Bn. H.Q. & "B" & "C" Coys. to GONNEHEM to rest & refit.	
LONG CORNET	24.4.15		Moved here to rear billets.	
	25 " "			
	26.4.15		Practically whole Battalion employed in trenching parties at RUG DU BOIS.	
RICHEBOURG St VAAST	27.4.15		Moved his into billets in Brigade Reserve.	
RICHEBOURG L'AVOUÉ	28.4.15		Occupied trenches in right centre section of D.3. 1 Company 9th King's transferred Bgt. attached to Bn H'Qr for march through. Relief completed in 1 hour 10 minutes. "A" Coy. (± 4½⅔) in front trench, "B" ± 75 to 200 his, "C" in support in day subs.	
	29.4.15		Front trenches knocked in early morning with minenwerfer — Heavy shelling about 5 p.m.	
	30.4.15		Front trenches knocked in — hostile provider & trench mortars attacked envergency rememberfer — Very heavy shelling from new to 1 pm, between 3 and 4 —	

Ted Vaughan
Lt Col
Comd. 5th Kc Liverp.

121/5 uuuu

2nd Brigade.

5th Royal Sussex.

Vol III 1 — 31.5.15.

C.3

Army Form C. 2118.

WAR DIARY
or
INTELLIGENCE SUMMARY.
(Erase heading not required.)

Instructions regarding War Diaries and Intelligence Summaries are contained in F.S. Regs., Part II. and the Staff Manual respectively. Title pages will be prepared in manuscript.

Place	Date	Hour	Summary of Events and Information	Remarks and references to Appendices
RICHEBOURG L'AVOUÉ	1.5.15	4.15 a.m / 5.30 a.m	Violent bombardment particularly of 2nd line & communication trenches during our 2 hours — Enemy at last silenced by our heavy artillery — C.S.M. Biggs mortally killed by a shell in his dug-out — Casualties remarkably slight — Men showed great steadiness under exceptionally heavy fire — Relieved by Scots Guards — (hundreds) (four rifles) 2/Lt. M.E. Price mortally killed by a rifle bullet outside his dug-out — handed during the night.	5/3
	2.5.15			
GONNEHEM	3.5.15	4.30 a.m	Arrived at 4.30 a.m. (Took over rest billets to before 2/Lt. Price buried in S.W. corner (under canopy) GONNEHEM Church-yard.)	
			Remained here until 6th. May when present order from present at —	
MESPLAUX	6.5.15 7.5.15	6 P.M	Move completed into above billets. Blank 1/15 4ths p. 1 P.Bns. when these have during the day. Bivouac orders to move off to RICHEBOURG L'AVOUÉ (arrived D.2) ready for attack at dawn on 8th. There commenced a steady Battalion forming (C Coy) behind Rue du Bois A.E. 10.15 (Sketch A.2) — moved into trenches at dawn.	
RICHEBOURG L'AVOUÉ	8.5.15			
	9.5.15	4 a.m	Heavy cannonade commenced on enemy's front & trenches raw and hostile positions — The Battalion had received orders to attack at 5.40 a.m after 10 minutes intense bombardment. The line of attack is shown in annexed sketch MAP. The orders as to attack were as follows — (Reference 1/LIFES — VIOLAINES — FESTUBERT 1/10000). The 2nd K.R.R. shown a Bn. to the left on Guards trench and the 1st. Northamptons on right, with right divided infront Q.2. The second line was the S.R. & Yorkshire Bn. on the left and the 2nd King's Royal Rifles on right. The third line were R.B. & lept the trench in Q.9 & Q.5 K.R.R supports in right. The 4th line (R.13) R.14 & between the trenches at the Round line between Q.2 & M.3 & when the last line had been taken by our line (R.10) — buildings about (R.13) — R.14 & between of over, making a strong point of the Farm at Q.10. The second line was ordered to clear the trenches, K.R.R. & R.R.R to work along R.8 perfect the right flank & eventually gain this orchard at R.14. One Battalion was to follow immediately in rear of the assaulting Battalions (East of Q.2) as necessary — clear all hostile trenches still occupied in rear of the assaulting Battalions. General reserves and ... of 3rd. ... from further in support — The Scott Guards & the Left Battalion the Irish Guards (Aubers) WELSH bullseye to (R.12, 13, 14, 15 & 16). One Battalion Queens & for Ab Co — the British 1st Battalion ...line EN.G. Corps B' AVOUÉ read from G.9 — P.8 — M.9 — M.25. One Battalion ordrs now for Aubers Bn. 9 & 15 C. Company on the left & from the first to second line of the Battalion, 2 pla B Company if the Battalion, ...	MAP A commenced. 1/10000 ILLIES VIOLAINES FESTUBERT

1577 Wt.W.6791/1773 500,000 1/15 D.D. & L. A.D.S.S./Forms/C. 2118.

Army Form C. 211

WAR DIARY or INTELLIGENCE SUMMARY.
(Erase heading not required.)

Place	Date	Hour	Summary of Events and Information	Remarks and references to Appendices
			into the enemy's trenches to work along trench to right in support of the left of the Mr Thompsons, the K.R.R. having by then moved right handed in their advance towards P8. The Battalion was ready in the O Lui & on the bombardment could moved A & O Coys into B-73 line, then followed across the open 150 yards to the advanced line after the 2/R.S. Sussex. Before reaching the advanced trench the Battalion had already suffered an extremely heavy [r?]/6, machine gun, & shell fire, — C Coy had 1 officer (2/Lt Haigh) wounded & about 30 men killed or wounded during this preliminary advance — C Company (less 1 Platoon) & A Company (less 1 Platoon) left in the front trenches & advanced most gallantly to the support of the 2nd Division, who were already held up by the enemy's fire — B Company (less 1 Platoon), having seen the left company of the K.R.R. go over the parapet, themselves went over & advanced a few rifle lgts [?]. Immediately stopped the 4th Platoon of A & B from advancing as I found the situation impossible & the men never could be advanced. The enemy's fire, particularly from machine guns and the ground in this schutzte [?] this line en our left flank, made it impossible for any one to advance. The men cut in front were lying flat constantly, the white parapet in front of the advanced trench showing their heads under our machine[?] & heavy shell fire. I found Lieuts Mant Capt Cresswell & Ainsley here with 30 odd of a Platoon of C Company from advancing — Lt Hopper was also wounded in the advance trench — At 7 a.m. orders were received to retire, & these men who could began to come in many of them wounded — Sly & Roberts were very brave in going out & houses who [?] orders to the firing line — Eventually no more orders that we could [?] understand temporarily — to collect our men in D.S. Line — but the ready to resume the attack on its [?] renewal after a further artillery bombardment — he then found 2/Lt R. Ingram had been killed, Major E. H. Langham, 2/Lt Smel, Perry, & Ahond, wounded & Capts Grant, Ahond [?] Price, & 2/Lt Proole remission were missing and about 2:30 the ranks within killed wounded or missing — About 2 p.m. we received orders from [?] to the 2 line in support billets 15th [?] Brigade, who were batched at 4:30. This Flag had — his attempt we trust that as far [?] as the Black Watch to some of the old 42nd. It was who got up against these extreme fire with him	5/3

Army Form C. 2118.

WAR DIARY
or
INTELLIGENCE SUMMARY.
(Erase heading not required.)

Instructions regarding War Diaries and Intelligence Summaries are contained in F. S. Regs., Part II. and the Staff Manual respectively. Title pages will be prepared in manuscript.

573-74

Place	Date	Hour	Summary of Events and Information	Remarks and references to Appendices
AVELETTE	10.5.15	8pm	Enemy's trenches may just got back, the attack failed as is the morning. At 8pm we were ordered to march to LE TOURET where we should get instructions as to billetting. The ground up to a little ?? Chocolat-Menier Corner, and Germans ?? & marched down in front through & constantly disorganized mass of men from other regiments. At LE TOURET we were ordered to go to Rhebo on which we stayed till 4 p.m. when we marched to	
GONNEHEN	11.5.15		and stayed there in rest till 16th until the next day when we moved to	
BETHUNE	12.5.15	5pm	[and took our billets in the Tobacco Factory in the Rue de Lille.] Remained there in Corps Reserve or than Brigade Reserve until the 20th 19th when the Battalion took ?? over from the French to reserve trench - S. of CUINCHY PERNELLES. We moved into Brigade support in front of the Battalion in the village in billets & A & B Coy & ?? B Coy in dug-outs near the MAISON ROUGE.	
CAMBRIN	20.5.15		Relieved 2 ?? A.C. Div in trench killing section Z, & into H9/2 near MAISON ROUGE. Capt. S?C	
" " "	24.5.15		Trans. officers temporary Adjutant, now Capt. ANTC dan to Hospital with nerve breakdown -	
	25.5.15		Brig-Coll. Maudsigned from before	
	27.5.15		Capt. E.R. temporarily nursing H/9/2 Q. Swan	
	28.5.15		Returned to billets in village in reliefs by ?? Sussex	
			Ordered to take over CUINCHY trenches tomorrow - left action from the CANAL knuckle & ALL	
	31.5.15		NIALL - Reinforcements of officers ?? hardly needed - moved to 6 company officers - about 360 ?? rifles for the front line - Total strength of 586 including 2 attached Officers, 2 ?N?, transport officers, P.M.O. -	

Reed S. Langham ?
Lieut Col
Comdg S.R. ??? Rgt —

1577 Wt W10711/1773 500,000 1/15 D.D.&L. A.D.S.S./Forms/C. 2118.

A

Attack plan   5th R¹ Sussex Reg¹
9th May 1915

FMS COUR D'AVOUÉ

GERMAN FRONT LINE

FME DU BOIS

M.G.

A line (front parapet)   D2
B line (2nd line)
RUE DU BOIS
C line (support)   D5 line
D3

C.4

121/5992

2nd Division

1/5th Sussex
Vol IV 1 — 27.6.15.

WAR DIARY or INTELLIGENCE SUMMARY

Army Form C. 2118.

Place	Date	Hour	Summary of Events and Information	Remarks and references to Appendices
CUINCHY	10.6.15		Relieved 1/ Northam E. in A3 :- from PALL MALL inclusive to the CANAL - B & C Companies in front trench, B & A Companies in support trenches - Very quiet trench on our own line - but 2 Enemy mines exploded on our right one being ½ minutes after on our left.	
BEUVRIÈRE	4.6.15 11 p.m / 8.6.15		at GIVENCHY on leaving the 3rd Tines. Relieved by 4/ R.W. Fusiliers & marched here to rest billets - Remainder in rest till Inspected by G.O.C. 1st Corps who spoke with of the Battalion in the Field, in billets on parade - Remainder are rest carrying out programme of work, route marches, target practice, musketry, field firing, ceremonial parades for disciplinary training - Stationary short of officers - Percy Sangerming as 1/t relieved last action on parade on 15th 4th ready Known as 1st of 111 NEW J section of trenches on 16th but to await further orders.	
OUESNOY	16.6.15		Moved into bivouacs in LE QUESNOY Wood (N.g. 15.cm.s)	
BUSNN	19.6.15		Moved into billets here - Draft of 9 officers arrived from England (including Lt. Thomas & 2/Lt. Kingse)	
LAVANTIE	24.6.15		Moved to Brigade Route March into billets here	
	26.6.15		Lieut SANSOM took over duties of Assistant	
BERGUNEUL	27.6.15		Moved into billets here - Working parties furnished to make new trench in rear of Z.I.	
	7.7.75			

Rudf.Langhun
Lt Col
Commanding 5/ Sussex

C.5

D/
6344

1/5 Invasion
Engagements

1/5th R. Sussex
Vol V 1 - 31.7.15

Army Form C. 2118.

WAR DIARY
or
INTELLIGENCE SUMMARY.
(Erase heading not required.)

Instructions regarding War Diaries and Intelligence Summaries are contained in F. S. Regs., Part II. and the Staff Manual respectively. Title pages will be prepared in manuscript.

Place	Date	Hour	Summary of Events and Information	Remarks and references to Appendices
MORVIGNEUL	1.7.15		In billets - See whilst	
LAMARIN	7.7.15		Took over Z.2. of CAMBRIN section of line from 9/Kings 3 Staffords - All four companies in front line. 1 Company & 2/ Sussex in SMS' KEEP & Supports & Reserve.	
VERQUIN	13.7.15		Relieved by 2/ Welch Regt and moved here into billets -	
VERMELLES	19.7.15		Took over Y.2. of VERMELLES section of line from London Scottish - A & B Coys in front line "D"s in support in Convoy Cromwell & "C" in Reserve in VERMELLES	
	21.7.15		"C" Company moved up to CARYL DUGOUTS	
	25.7.15		"D" Company relieved "A" in front line	
LA BOURSE	25.7.15		Trench took two hits by bullets - No casualties - During this 6 days in trenches Working hrs to X3 front by day & usual by night to complete CHAPEL ALLEY	
	27.7.15		Jumpers near line 400 yds long to be Nun trench between Y.1 - Y.2 - Work continued till 30 July. nightly.	
GARDEN CITY	31.7.15		Moved here to complete & to hand this new Camp.	

Reed Caughey
Lt.C.A.
2/ Sussex.

WAR DIARY
or
INTELLIGENCE SUMMARY.
(Erase heading not required.)

Army Form C. 2118.

Instructions regarding War Diaries and Intelligence Summaries are contained in F. S. Regs., Part II. and the Staff Manual respectively. Title pages will be prepared in manuscript.

Place	Date	Hour	Summary of Events and Information	Remarks and references to Appendices
GARDEN CITY	1.8.15		Continued work on tent camp — made roads — erected Orderly Room & Officers' quarters — made 3 new bridges on 6 footbridges — dug out & completed swimming camp huts — put in overhead grazing over indoor camp — small hill	
SAILLY LA BOURSE	6.8.15		Moved here to Brigade Reserve in huts. Heard that Kitchener Orchestra from where informant came were miserable & unworkable. The result was that they were disregarded & troops to VERMELLES & MAZINGARBE was made disregarded.	
CAMBRIN	8.8.15		Relieved 7/K.R. Rens in trenches section Z.1.	
ANNEQUIN	12.8.15		Relieved by 9/Kings Kingsford — Fired during my wife M.G. in HAINES with materials for an main street. (range 3100 yds & elsewhere) & also on 2' of 3rd line trenches in QUINCHY TRIANGLE (range 1800 yds). Some shelling at 5. my neuralgic direction a position in 2° line whose M.G. Gen had first in evening — in order by cross hairing from HAINES & QUINCHY, is a must leave done damage — The shells each one as approximately a shot by of 4.2 shrapnel with reasonable explosive — very many a high tk had nickelium at last reports with few another. Handed KMB to ANNEQUIN	
"	17.8.15		Mostly trenches in now Support trench in Z.1. T. Kept me trenches in RAILWAY ALLEY, on 2nd line defence at CAMBRIN & ANNEQUIN. Warned file ready of entrance for III Army left attacks K.p.F. & tr.	
FOUQUEREUIL	18.8.15		Relieved by 4/K.R.R. 7.30" & marched here — 6th detach approved. Inspected by G.O.C. 1st Army & G.G.C. 2/Brigade — Told he may be found his PIONEERS. In now congratulated to indays having played the game." while with the Division — exactly 6 months.	
"	19.9.15		Continued at 3.15 p.m. & arrived here all 9.16 am internet transet to when we arrive shot 4 a.m. Told no more situation repartoirs war. PIONEER Kentington	
DOULLENS STRETON LOUVENCOURT	20.9.15 24.9.15 "		Marched here at 2.15 from 5 HQrs & Arts by to next into Village — Crd by knedr. (apt A HUWOOD) must a reduction duty to CALINCAMPS Kpatrly LA SIGNY Farm.	
—	22.9.15		Nearly in his duty in RAISES WARRIMONT (near ACHE'16).	
"	25.9.15		The 2 bys in independent march to SAILLY-au-BOIS — on change of Divisional Boundaries —	

Army Form C. 2118.

WAR DIARY
or
INTELLIGENCE SUMMARY.
(Erase heading not required.)

Instructions regarding War Diaries and Intelligence Summaries are contained in F. S. Regs., Part II. and the Staff Manual respectively. Title pages will be prepared in manuscript.

Place	Date	Hour	Summary of Events and Information	Remarks and references to Appendices
SAILLY-AU-BOIS	29/8/15		H"qrs & Arts'Grps moved here. Rifires working parties daily on SAILLY ditches from MILL at COLINCAMPS northwards in front of SAILLY to point due N. of CH" de la HAIE, & on the SAILLY village defences	

Rad Vaughan
Lt. Col.
Comm'd St. R. Thames Rgt.

5/ Royal Sussex.

August 1915

Transferred to
48th Div. as
Pioneers 20.8.15

France
5 Bn 2 Bde 1st Div
16 Feb - 9 Aug 1915